# NEVER HAD A JOB: LIVING THE DREAM OF ENTREPRENEURSHIP

Written By: Kyle Hiersche

Edited By: Kraig Hiersche, Nick Hiersche & Vickie Saula

*Dedicated to my sons;*
*Julian and Christian.*

# ACKNOWLEDGMENT

I would like to start this book by recognizing some of the people that helped me get to the surreal point of being able to write a book like this. While I am passionate about the advice and examples in this book, they alone would not have led me to the success I have seen. I owe many of my accomplishments to the amazing support system I've had in my life starting with both of my parents, all four of my grandparents, and of course my brother and business partner, Nick.

I would like to thank my best friends Corey John, Brianna, and Danny Mixtape for their guidance and support. They say you are only as good as the company you keep and I have had amazing people in my life that have contributed to my success, so I am grateful for every one of them.

# INTRODUCTION

At the age of 31, I have never had a job working for someone else in my life. As an entrepreneur that had an early start, I am fortunate enough to only have worked for myself. My businesses have taken me around the world to places I could only have dreamed of as a kid. When I founded my first company at the age of 15, I had no idea it would change my life in so many amazing ways. I am very blessed to be living the American dream, the entrepreneur's dream.

This book will share some of the knowledge, insight, and lessons that I have learned on my 16-year journey as an entrepreneur thus far. I broke it down to 30 short chapters because let's face it...who has time to read a thousand pages anyway? These are my 30 tips for all entrepreneurs, especially young ones looking to start their journey.

# CHAPTER 1:
# START EARLY

While I realize it may be too late for some people reading this to start your entrepreneurial endeavors as early as I did, you can still start now. You can also still spread this mindset to future generations starting with your loved ones, children, or grandchildren.

Starting early was by far the biggest advantage I had as an entrepreneur. Everyone says, "You have to fail your way to the top." So I think it's better to start failing when you have the least to risk...during childhood. If you can try your hand at creating your first few businesses before adulthood, chances are one of them will succeed enough for you to pursue it. That is exactly what I did.

By the time I graduated high school, I was seeing enough income and light at the end of the tunnel to work full time on my dream. Some of my family thought I was crazy for not going to college, but I was already working full time for myself.  Fast forward 13 years later and I continue to work for myself full time.

# CHAPTER 1 QUICK TIPS

- Don't wait for investors or venture capital. That will just hold you back from getting started. We have never waited on investors or received venture capital.

- Be your own investor. If you believe in yourself, put your money where your mouth is.

- Do what you can, when you can. The key is to start now and be consistent.

- Every day that you wait, you are another day further from living your dream.

# CHAPTER 2:
# WORK HARD

The crux of this book and the biggest reason for my success is working hard.  There really is no way around this if you want to be successful, the work never stops.  Particularly in our generation, everyone wants the cheat code to success without the hard work.  The truth is... there just isn't one.

In my experience, hard work and dedication is the only road to success unless you are going to sit around and wait to win the lottery (literally or metaphorically). Of course, there are exceptions when people get lucky and are successful right out of the gate, especially in today's viral world. Even if you get lucky and have a product go viral out of the gate, you still need to have the infrastructure, the follow-up, and the work ethic to turn that into a lasting business.

According to the Small Business Administration, only four out of five establishments that started in 2017 survived until 2018 (79.4%). Only ⅓ of businesses will survive 10 years or longer.[1] It will take hard work and an extreme belief in your company to become one that survives the first years and eventually becomes a profitable endeavor.

So, how can you possibly work hard enough to build your business from scratch while still trying to pay your bills and live your life? Well to start, let's think about all of the extra things in your life that are not contributing to your dreams or what is vital to your life. How many TV shows do you watch? How many times do you go out on the weekends? How many times have you slept in and just been lazy around the house? Those are all things that everyone does, including me, but those are also key times that we could spend working on our business.

In today's world, by using your computer or phone you can be working on your business from anywhere, at any time. You don't need to plan a meeting or have an office to take your business ventures seriously and work on them. You can work 24/7 or in between juggling a full-time job and school. You now have the power to manifest your own destiny anytime from any location.

Stop making excuses and start seizing every free moment of time to build your dream because that is what dreamers do. I love the quote from the late great Jim Rohn when he says "Rest very little...Make rest a necessity, not an objective. The objective of life is not to rest, the objective of life is to act."

# CHAPTER 2 QUICK TIPS

- Start replacing leisure time with time spent working on your dream.

- Use your phone or computer to work from wherever you can, whenever you can.

- We all have the same 24 hours in a day. What you do with yours makes the difference.

# CHAPTER 3:
# RESOURCES

This chapter is very much a testament to how blessed I am to have such amazing people in my life that have helped me get to this point. While I appreciate them and everyone who has ever worked with me, people did not just jump out of nowhere and offer to help me or work with me to build MY dream.

There have been a few times lately where people have told me "I'm trying to do this but you know... I don't have a whole team behind me like you do" as if that's an excuse before they even try! It is frustrating for an entrepreneur to hear that, because none of us had a team at one point in time. We all started with just a dream and the passion to pursue that dream.

I have had many staff members, but none of them have ever volunteered to work for me for free. They do a specific job that I have laid out for them for an agreed upon amount of compensation. Anyone can hire an employee when the time is right. Before we get to that point though, we need to use all the resources we already have at our disposal.

When it comes to using your resources, think of anyone in your family or circle of friends that does something that you need as a part of your business and utilize your relationship with them to get those services highly discounted. Do you have any friends or family members that are accountants, web designers, salespeople? Have you been to a conference or event where you met someone and formed a relationship? These types of people will help you throughout your journey.

Put in the work to show people you are serious about your business and some will help you, maybe even for free in the beginning. What they will not do is jump out of nowhere and volunteer to build your dream for you.

# CHAPTER 3 QUICK TIPS

## Human Resources For Entrepreneurs Whom You May Already Know:

- Business Partners

- Accountants

- Attorneys

- Web Developers

- Graphic Designers

- Sales People

- Realtors

- General Contractors

- Insurance Agents

# CHAPTER 4: FIND A PARTNER

I was very blessed to have my only sibling as my business partner, my brother Nick. He happens to balance me with strengths, weaknesses, and thinking from different perspectives. This allows us to focus on our areas of strength so our businesses can get the best from both of us.

He ended up graduating college with a business degree and has used his education to help our businesses immensely. I on the other hand, did not attend college but possess many of the entrepreneurial traits that he lacks. We compliment each other.

Through our years of partnership, my brother and I have had our ups, downs and many heated arguments. We are siblings after all. Through all of this, I have always appreciated our balance in the realm of business. I wouldn't trade it for the world and neither of us start ventures without the other.

Having a partner means someone is always there to

bounce ideas off and brainstorm strategies. You need someone who is just as excited as you are when you call them at 3 AM and say "I got it! I had a stroke of genius!". No one is going to be as excited to talk to you about your business than someone who is equally involved. Without talking about them, you can't really conceptualize ideas and turn them into reality. That is exactly why, in my opinion, a partner is key.

# CHAPTER 4 QUICK TIPS

- Partner with someone who can fully commit to the business and is as "all in" as you are.

- A great partner is someone who can complement your strengths and weaknesses.

- Finding a partner that you can trust is key, but real trust is built over time.

- Remember to appreciate your business partners and be a good partner yourself. Listen to ideas and work together so the business benefits from all partners.

# CHAPTER 5: OWN THE REAL ESTATE

In my opinion, the smartest moves that my brother and I have made as businessmen is to own the real estate behind the businesses that we run. Purchasing the offices that our businesses operate out of has been key. Not only does owning real estate build real wealth, but it also allows you to be extremely flexible as an entrepreneur.

If your business fails or falls on hard times, you can use the space to create another business or lease some of the space to fill that income gap. If times get hard, of course, you can sell the real estate to get your capital out of it and start a new venture.

Bottom line is, if your business is paying rent to yourself as the landlord then it's a win/win. Another advantage is that real estate usually increases in value and is a great investment in general. You know what they say, "Buy land because they aren't making any more of it."

Owning the real estate that your business operates from gives a greater purpose to your business, even if it's spinning wheels trying to make a profit. If you can pay the rent to yourself, you come out ahead in the long run by building equity in the real estate, regardless of how successful the underlying business is. I recommend doing this as soon as your business and income allows you to which means you may have to sacrifice taking out profits for a while to set this up.

A great resource that we utilized to help our business purchase our first office was the Small Business Administration. The SBA can help you finance a commercial location for as little as 10% down if your income supports the purchase. Financing that can be provided by the SBA and other sources are another reason to make sure your income is on the books and reported properly.

I suggest that any U.S. business owner explores what the SBA can do for them and their business. It was created by the United States government to help small businesses and has ample financing to do so. It will take a good amount of paperwork and jumping through hoops, but it's all worth it in the end, trust me.

I would also recommend getting your real estate license in your state. Every state's requirements are different, and some are harder than others, but none of them are really difficult or expensive. Being a licensed Realtor allows you access to real estate information that you would not have otherwise. This allows you to make smarter real estate plays and to buy and sell your own properties without paying commissions.

# CHAPTER 5 QUICK TIPS

- Use resources like the Small Business Administration to purchase business locations.

- Use the money you would pay for a lease to pay yourself rent and build equity.

- Before launching new ventures, target the real estate behind that venture first.

- Get your real estate license so you can buy and sell your own properties.

- Always purchase real estate based on the golden rule; location, location, location!

# CHAPTER 6: DON'T BE PICKY

When I was 10 years old, I wanted to be a musician and I couldn't imagine a life being anything else. The music business is very difficult and expensive to pursue, so my first businesses were always intended to provide a budget for my music career. Those businesses began taking me further and further away from the dream of being a musician. I had caught the entrepreneurial bug.

By the age of 18, I was a full-time entrepreneur that could really care less about being a musician anymore. I was making money doing what I loved because it was a business that I created. I love all of my businesses because I was involved in the creation of them, they are like my children. Just because they don't always match my initial "dream" or "passion" does not mean I don't love them or that I failed at my dream. It just means that my dreams have changed.

I remember a quote from Mark Cuban where he

said: "You should be following your efforts." I think that really sums up this chapter and what I am trying to get across here. You have to have an open mind as an entrepreneur and follow where the business and money takes you. More than anything though, follow your efforts to where it is working. If something is working and shows promise as a business, you have to pursue that regardless of what your original dream was. Follow your efforts, and let your efforts follow the money.

# CHAPTER 6 QUICK TIPS

- Keep an open mind to go where the business takes you. Success never happens as originally planned.

- Pay attention to what works in the market and follow that path. Money talks.

- Aim, fire, aim, fire. You can adjust as you go, but first you need to get going!

# CHAPTER 7: NO PLAN B

T he best mindset to have, is to act as if you have no backup plan. I have no idea what I would be doing if I weren't an entrepreneur. I never went to college so I can't imagine it would be very exciting or well paying. Failing has never been an option for me. Success has always been the only option, which is why I have never stopped or taken no for an answer.

I am in no way telling you to quit your job or school. I believe you should give your all into everything you do. When it comes to your business, you must act as if failing is not an option. Without that fire inside of you, there is no way to endure the cold world of entrepreneurship when it slaps you in the face repeatedly.

Whether you are in the startup phase or trying to maintain a successful business, you will go through trying times that will test your will and dedication in every way. It's the one-track mindset of not having a Plan B that will get you through those times and push you to a better place. There's something about having a backup option that consciously or subconsciously affects your hunger and work ethic. Cut the backup plan, make this the only option and you will have no choice but to succeed.

I have never had a job in my life. I have never filled out a job application, never clocked in one hour of work for someone else. I know for a fact that I will not fail as an entrepreneur... I have no other choice.

# CHAPTER 7 QUICK TIPS

- Act as if failure is not an option. There is no going back to a job.

- Don't take no for an answer. Do whatever it takes and convince whoever it takes to make it happen.

- Ditch the backup plans. If you believe in yourself then don't give yourself an option.

- Go hard or go home...literally. For entrepreneurs, it has to be all or nothing.

# CHAPTER 8: SELL BEFORE YOU BUY

This concept, like many others in this book, is not original to me and has been preached by many over the years. It is something that has been used in sales and entrepreneur training for decades. The idea is to sell or fund something before you have to produce or deliver this product or service. In essence... making something out of nothing.

When I was 18, I started what would become one of my most lucrative ventures. This new idea required some funding that we did not have at the time. Instead, I found a way to sell the product before I actually had it. I had sold someone part of something that was planned out but did not actually exist yet. Once I received the money, I completed the product and delivered it. I was up and running with that new idea and knew if it worked once, it would work again.

# CHAPTER 8 QUICK TIPS

- Find ways to sell your products or services before having to invest capital into them.

- You can use crowdfunding sites like Kickstarter and Gofundme to get future customers to fund the development and manufacturing of your product.

- Test the marketplace with potential sales before even investing time in pursuing an idea.

# CHAPTER 9: PAY YOUR FEES

W hen you do start selling products or services, you need to make sure you pay your own fees. This chapter is really about a pet peeve of mine that I see small businesses do. It's now 2020, so if your business does not accept credit cards or electronic forms of payment then you are not serious about your business. At the same time, if you accept cards but then pass your payment processing fees on to your customers...then you are just as bad.

Payment processing fees are to be paid by the seller and should never be passed on to the consumer, ever. Your prices need to be set so that the payment processing fees can be covered by the base price of your product or service. The only thing that should be added to the price is taxes of course, when applicable.

Paying fees to receive payments is just part of the game, especially in today's digital world. It is just a cost that you are going to incur as a business, and you have to look at it in a positive light. Paying the payment processing fees and taking that hit is allowing your business the best possible chance to succeed by not denying any customers or payments. It is 2020, cash is irrelevant and in the world of credit cards and online payment processing, you have to pay to play.

Here is a quick look at the current biggest payment processors, their fees, and Pros and Cons of each.

# CHAPTER 9 QUICK TIPS

## Payment Processor Comparisons:

| Payment Processor | Paypal | Stripe | Square |
|---|---|---|---|
| **Online Fee** | 2.9% + $0.30 | 2.9% + $0.30 | 2.6% + $0.10 |
| **Card Reader Fee** | 2.7% - 3.5% | Not Available | 2.75% |
| **Pros** | Trusted Brand | Simplest Checkout | Lowest Fee |
| **Cons** | Pushes users to sign up for membership instead of focusing on pushing them through the payment process seamlessly. | Takes longer to receive funds than Paypal | Online checkout not as stream-lined as others |

# CHAPTER 10:
# REINVEST

As an entrepreneur, investment capital is vital to the survival of your ventures and therefore to your own survival. It's for this reason that you must always be your own investor and reinvest money back into your business. I believe that not reinvesting is a mistake that a lot of entrepreneurs make and it leads to them failing in the long run. It's particularly important to reinvest in the beginning of the journey. That is the fuel that your business will need to turn your initial spark into a fire.

In our early years, it was a very long time before we ever took a paycheck. We had built the business to the point of relocating to Miami, leasing an office and hiring four full-time staff members before actually paying ourselves a real paycheck. The company was making money, but we were using that to pay more employees and grow the business instead of paying ourselves. That is reinvesting.

Some of my business peers make the mistake of not reinvesting vigorously and then wonder why my business is steadily increasing while theirs is decreasing. The answer is simple... I reinvested the profits so the business could grow and then reinvest to grow even more. This is a cycle that continues and as it gets bigger you can start to take a little bit more profits or salary...but the cycle always continues. You must be making more than enough income to reinvest in the business heavily before taking more profits out.

In conclusion, your business needs to be making a healthy amount before you actually start taking real profits or salaries from the business. Even when you do, it needs to be relative to the amount that you are still reinvesting back into the business so that the cycle never stops. In my opinion, most reinvesting should be done in advertising.

# CHAPTER 10
# QUICK TIPS

- Reinvest profits back into the business until you can afford to take a real paycheck

- Always continue the cycle of reinvesting before taking paychecks, no matter how big the company gets

- Reinvest in advertising first and foremost - there will never be any money to take paychecks without new customers.

# CHAPTER 11:
# ADVERTISE

The most important investment to make for a business hands down is advertising. Henry Ford famously said, "A man who stops advertising to save money is like a man who stops a clock to save time." I couldn't agree with you more Henry! I have always lived by this and have always invested heavily into advertising. Those investments have always paid off for me.

There were times in our business where we had absolutely no money to pay ourselves or other bills, but our Google Ads or whatever method we were using to advertise were never touched. We would never even think about cutting the advertising budget because if we did, then how would we ever get paychecks again? Where would the money come from to pay our bills if we stopped acquiring new customers through advertising?

Investing in advertising can be more than just

spending money, it really comes down to finding where your customers are and getting your message to them. In today's landscape that can mean reaching them through social media, email, or a variety of other new methods. Sometimes it can be a free promotion that just took some time and effort to create, especially if something goes viral on social media.

Newer advertising platforms like Facebook allow you to target your exact audience and serve them the exact content or ads that you choose for whatever budget you would like to spend. You no longer need to have a gigantic TV or Billboard budget to advertise your business. There is no excuse to not advertise. The days of paying to be in the phone book are over. Everyone is listed on Google for free, so it is up to you to get good reviews and advertise to get more customers.

# CHAPTER 11
# QUICK TIPS

## Key Advertising Platforms:

- Facebook
- Instagram
- Email Newsletters
- Google Ads

# CHAPTER 12:
# NETWORK

Networking is just as important as advertising because you are going to need the people in your network to help you get to the next level. That applies to everything from putting together your product or service, getting it out to the public, and executing it once it's sold. One of my mentors J Hatch always says, "Your net worth is only as big as your network" which we still say at all of our events, all around the world.

It really doesn't matter what industry you are in; networking is key. When I was younger, I used to attend every music conference I possibly could because that was the industry I was in at the time. Not only was I learning much of the knowledge that I needed to start some of my businesses, but I was meeting many of the people that I needed to know to start those businesses.

The people that I met at those conferences were key to building my entire first business and changed my life. One of the conferences that I attended was in

Miami and it was the first time that I had been to Miami. Within 3 weeks of getting home from that conference, my brother and I had signed a lease for a condo in Miami and moved our entire operation from Portland. Attending that one conference in Miami changed my life forever. Who knows where I would be if I had not attended that conference to increase my knowledge and network.

Almost every industry has multiple conferences all over the world. I would recommend attending as many as you can, especially if you're starting a new business. When we first relocated our company to Miami, we used to buy everyone drinks to network. Whether it was buying drinks at the hotel bar, at a conference, or bottles in the nightclubs, we used to buy everyone drinks as a way to break the ice. Trust me, it worked like a charm.

I can't stress enough how important networking has been to my career and still is to this day. I still attend conferences all around the world every year. I also still buy everyone drinks at the conferences as often as possible! Your net worth is only as big as your network, so get out there and get your network on!

# CHAPTER 12
# QUICK TIPS

- Be where the people are. Put yourself in a position to network with the people you need.

- Stay clean and presentable.

- Bring something to the table. Break the ice with drinks, food or something else so they want to network with you.

- Stay consistent. People need to see you a few times to get to know you.

# CHAPTER 13:
# TEST IDEAS

T esting an idea is the only way to find out if it will work. You can speculate in your mind over and over, but putting it out there into the marketplace is the only way to truly know. All of our businesses have come about from testing different small ideas to see if they work. If they work, we can begin to build a business around them. Once we have a business going, we "follow our efforts" and continue to test new ideas.

Running a business involves constantly trying new ideas whether it's a new product, service, or business strategy. It could even be a new way to communicate with clients to increase your conversion rate or get them more involved with your brand.

There are many reasons why testing ideas comes in handy in the business world, but you need the right data from your test. The key is to follow the winners and revise the losers. It is a constant game of trial and error which can be fun for you and your team if you look at it that way. There are even services such as VWO that allow you to A/B test different versions of your site or conversion pages. You can design new versions of your site and see which designs drive your customers in the best way.

My business partners and I are constantly taking advantage of lunches together and weekend gatherings to talk about testing new ideas. Sometimes it's hard to spend time out of your actual workday to talk about new ideas to implement. I suggest trying it at lunch with some colleagues because it really works great for us.

New technology empowers entrepreneurs to test ideas and receive instant feedback like never before. You can take an idea, make a landing page, create a graphic, write some copy, put an ad on Facebook to your demographic to test it...all in the same day. Let's just take a second to think about how amazing that is. Now let's not take it for granted!

If you asked my brother or myself to paraphrase what running a business is, we would probably say that it's "problem-solving and trying things." In my experience, it is true because our biggest ventures have come from one of many ideas that we just tried. We tested, saw that they worked a little and pursued them more. It takes a lot of testing to get where you want to be, so start trying things now!

# CHAPTER 13
# QUICK TIPS

- Constantly test new ideas, advertising and conversion methods using as much data as possible.

- Use Facebook Ads to send customers to your test and gather data.

- A/B test your website and conversion pages with tools like VWO (Visual Web Optimizer) www.vwo.com

- Track your consumer's behavior with website heatmap trackers such as www.hotjar.com

# CHAPTER 14:
# COMPETITION

A s an entrepreneur, doing research on your competition and your market is vital. I am amazed by
the number of people that put in huge amounts
of work for an idea without simply using Google. Typ-
ing in a few words on Google can bring you all the research you need, yet many people fail to do this simple
exercise

I especially see this with people not researching
their competition. People will assume an idea they
have is original or that there is no competition without
even doing the simple task of Googling the competition. Researching competition should be the very first
part of an idea.

If you have thought of something, chances are
other people have thought of that too and are already
out there doing it. If you do the quick legwork of scour-
ing Google and you don't see any competition, then you
are really in business. If you do see competition, that's

okay too. Most business ideas are already going to have some type of competitors out there, but that is where the research allows you to win.

Being able to look up your competition and see what they're doing before you even launch is an amazing aspect of entrepreneurship in the digital age. Almost everything about a business and their process is online in some way for you to find, dissect and learn from. This is how you find the gaps in the market that need to be filled. This is what you base your business on, learning from the strengths and weaknesses of competition. It's so simple in today's market and so vital to success. It's really amazing to me that so many people don't go through this simple process.

# CHAPTER 14
# QUICK TIPS

- Google your competition. A simple search can tell you a lot.

- If there is competition, investigate them thoroughly; strengths and weaknesses.

- Research the size of the market; are people talking about the need for this idea already online?

- Search social media names and hashtags to find anything that's out there already related to the idea.

# CHAPTER 15:
# RESEARCH COST

After researching the competition of a new idea, the next step is to simply calculate your costs of trying the idea on the most basic level. How much time and money is it going to take for you to get the most rudimentary version of the idea up and running? Without calculating the cost and time in advance, you have no idea if it's even possible to bring it to life in the real world.

Some ideas that people come to me with have had minimal thought put into them. People will suggest something without the knowledge of what it would take to implement it. I am not suggesting you don't listen to other people's ideas or follow your own, but there must be a structure to the process.

As you practice researching the competition and the cost for each idea you have, this will become ingrained in your entrepreneur mind. It will eventually get to the point that before even saying an idea out loud or putting it on paper, you can go through this process in your head and decide if it's even plausible.

This process has killed many ideas for my business partners and me before they even had a chance to live, but that is how the game goes. If you just ran around trying every idea you ever thought of without structure, then you would have no money or time to focus on building any one business.

# CHAPTER 15
# QUICK TIPS

- What is it going to cost to try the most basic versions of an idea to test it?

- What costs would you incur when eventually scaling the idea to full size?

- Are the costs of trying out the idea or scaling it to full size worth the potential payoff?

- Can you afford to test the idea now? If not, work on the basics to create the capital needed to try the idea.

# CHAPTER 16: STAY FOCUSED

Keeping your "eyes on the prize" and staying focused is key for an entrepreneur, especially since we tend to have a lot of ideas to try. I mean, we are entrepreneurs, aren't we? So how do you stay focused enough to build a business while still having that entrepreneurial streak inside of you? That is a question that many of us struggle with daily.

For me, it helps to stay focused on the current business by keeping in mind that the new ideas I want to try are going to take capital to attempt correctly. A lot of times, that fires me up to work harder on my current businesses. I like to use the excitement of a new idea to work even harder so that I can be able to try the new idea as soon as possible.

To attempt a new idea for another business you are going to need capital and time, so it is going to take a lot of work to be able to do that while maintaining enough attention to your current business. You are going to have to make more money, maybe even hire a new employee, and train them to do some of the tasks that you currently do so you can have time for the new idea.

This all takes time, effort and planning to pull off. In the meantime, you will see if your enthusiasm about the new idea was just a flash in the pan or if the excitement really holds the test of time. While you are in this process, you can also use that time to do some market research regarding your new idea.

# CHAPTER 16
# QUICK TIPS

- Keep in mind that most successful entre-preneurs have seen most of their early success from one business.

- New businesses take time and capital to execute.  Stay focused on the business at hand to create that extra time and capital needed.

- While waiting for the right time to try new ideas, you will see if the excitement of an idea holds true.

- Stay focused on the big picture and never forget to do the little things that add up to big wins.

# CHAPTER 17: THE LITTLE THINGS

As an entrepreneur it is easy to get distracted by ideas of grandeur because that is what we do, we are dreamers. However, we must remember to do the little things that need to be done every day in order to turn our dreams into realities. The little things matter and add up in a big way.

We all know someone who has seen a product and said, "I thought about that years ago! I should be rich!" No, they should not be rich. They didn't put in the work or do the little daily tasks needed to turn that idea into the product. Winning entrepreneurs are not those that think of good ideas, they are those that do the work necessary to bring those ideas to the world.

A great way to grasp the importance of doing the little things is by reading a book that changed my life when I read it. The book is called *The Slight Edge* by Jeff Olson and I always recommend it to anyone looking to better their life, not just in business. Using examples like the powers of compound interest and doubling, the book explains the importance of how doing little things every single day add up to make a huge impact over time.

What if you read ten pages of a book that you can learn from every day? How many books would you have read five years from now? How much more knowledge would you possess to apply to your business? The power of compounding simple tasks every day over time is amazing and can be applied to your health, knowledge, business, and any other aspect of your life.

Simple daily disciplines that are easy to do can have huge results over the course of time. The problem is if you never start them, then you will never see the compounded effects of them.

# CHAPTER 17
# QUICK TIPS

- The little things add up in a big way. Never underestimate the power of small daily tasks.

- Read *The Slight Edge* by Jeff Olson to understand the power of small daily disciplines over time.

- Read at least ten pages of a good book every day - over time the results will amaze you.

- Map out small daily disciplines that you can commit to every single day and use the compounding power of time.

# CHAPTER 18: FIND YOUR LANE

Finding your lane in the business world translates to finding a niche for your business. Find your lane and ride it until the wheels fall off! Creating a business with the right niche can mean that competition either does not exist yet or is effectively rendered irrelevant by your unique offering. A book that gives great insight into this is *Blue Ocean Strategy* by W. Chan Kim & Renee Mauborgne.

My brother read *Blue Ocean Strategy* in business school and then gave me a copy of it. It's a fascinating book and poses the idea that instead of competing in the "red ocean" that is bloody from competition, it is best to create an entirely new industry and therefore swim in the "blue ocean". It uses many examples of how this has been done in the past by everyone from businesses like Cirque du Soleil to city Police Chiefs. It is a very interesting and pertinent book to this point; I suggest giving it a read.

Finding your "lane" or "niche" is easier said than done, no matter how many college textbooks you have read. That is where brainstorming, research, and testing come in to save the day! Take your original ideas as an entrepreneur and put them through the brainstorming process with your partner.

Research if there is any competition. If so, find their strengths and weaknesses. What are you going to do to have a niche in this market? Then start implementing these by trial and error, go with what works and repeat the process. When going through this trial and error process, it's always best to try the simplest form of the idea first so you can test it before spending too much time and money.

# CHAPTER 18
# QUICK TIPS

- Find your niche for your business. What sets you apart from others?

- Double down on your uniqueness. Own your differences and show the market why that makes you better than the competition.

- Read books like *The Blue Ocean Strategy* to get your wheels turning on finding your lane.

- Research your competition or lack thereof. This data is priceless for entrepreneurs.

# CHAPTER 19:
# START SIMPLE

I must admit that to this day my Dad still reminds me to start with the simplest possible form of an idea to test it at first. This is something called the Minimal Viable Product taken from the book *The Lean Startup* by Eric Ries. The definition of the Minimal Viable Product is "that version of a new product a team uses to collect the maximum amount of validated learning about customers with the least effort."

The Minimal Viable Product is what you need to implement any new idea, strategy or even a whole business venture. In the digital age, this is simpler than ever using social media, websites, conversion rates, and being able to figure out your customer acquisition cost. You can put out a basic version of an idea, blast it on social media pushing customers to a site and figure out your conversion rate all in the same day. It really is an exciting time to be in business and entrepreneurs need to take advantage of it!

Take a little time to break down your big ideas into smaller simpler ideas and put out tests of them as feelers. Make sure you break them down into processes that are taking the least amount of money and resources to test. Then you can go out and test it, even test as many as you can! You must keep trying things!

# CHAPTER 19
# QUICK TIPS

- Always start with the simplest form of an idea to test. The "Minimal Viable Product"

- Invest the least amount of time and resources into an idea before testing and getting data.

- Break down bigger ideas into smaller actions to test easily.

- Use the data of the test to determine if the idea is worth pursuing or tweaking.

# CHAPTER 20:
# "TV" TO "ED"

Replacing the time you would normally spend watching TV with time spent working on your dream is key. However, like we talked about in the Work Hard chapter, you can also turn the Television into education. What I mean by that is that we all relax and watch some TV from time to time, but you can also watch something that's educational and entertaining.

There are many shows now on television and online that are for or about entrepreneurs and business people. My personal favorites to watch are *The Profit* and *Shark Tank*. The way that "The Profit" Marcus Lemonis is able to deal with people is an inspiration for me to be a better manager and business person every time I watch it. The entrepreneurs and new ideas on Shark Tank get me excited about running my business and usually make me jump up and get right back to work when the show ends.

Some entrepreneur TV shows are better and more

"real" than others, but they all bring some sort of inspiration or motivation that you can apply to your business. Enjoying these shows can turn recreational TV time into learning and motivational time so that you can charge up to tackle more tasks with a positive attitude.

# CHAPTER 20
# QUICK TIPS

**Entrepreneurial/Business Television Series:**

- *Titans* (CNBC)

- *Shark Tank* (ABC)

- *The Profit* (CNBC)

- *Follow The Leader* (CNBC)

- *Billion Dollar Buyer* (CNBC)

- *The Men Who Built America* (History)

- *Bloomberg Risk Takers* (Bloomberg TV)

# CHAPTER 21:
# POSITIVE VIBES

K eeping a positive attitude when you're constantly being beaten down is a daunting task for entrepreneurs. Even as I sit here writing this during a trying time in my life, my will to stay positive is being tested. How will I manage to stay positive in the most stressful times in my life? Listening to motivational speaking is what works best to keep me in a positive mindset.

Some of my personal favorite motivational speakers are Jim Rohn, Zig Ziglar, Gary V, and Tony Robbins. Nowadays you don't even have to read books, you can just type in any one of those names on YouTube and a plethora of videos will come up. In one click you can play any of them and get a massive dose of motivation and knowledge...for free!

The positive attitude these speeches create allows you to brush off the negativity and hate coming your way. They make you feel as though you have been lifted to a new level of entrepreneurial superpower. A superpower that makes it possible for you to get more done than you ever thought you could with laser focus and zero doubt. However, this will not last forever, as nothing does.

The late great Zig Ziglar was quoted to have said "People often say that motivation doesn't last. Well, neither does bathing - that's why we recommend it daily." A very true statement here, you need motivation constantly to stay positive and make it through the tough times. So, when I need someone to pull me up, I turn to the motivational speakers that are always right there in my pocket.

# CHAPTER 21
# QUICK TIPS

## Great Positive Quotes:

- "It's Not the Blowing of the Wind that Determines Your Destination, It's the Set of the Sail. The Same Wind Blows on us All." - Jim Rohn

- "Positive thinking will let you do everything better...than negative thinking will." - Zig Ziglar

- "Once you replace negative thoughts with positive ones, you'll start having positive results." - Willie Nelson

- "Believe you can and you're halfway there." - Theodore Roosevelt

- "What we think, we become." - Buddha

- "I hated every minute of training, but I said, 'Don't quit. Suffer now and live the rest of your life as a champion.'" - Muhammad Ali

- "Do the thing and you will have the power." - Ralph Waldo Emerson

# CHAPTER 22: DO THE THING

There is a famous quote from Ralph Waldo Emerson that says, "Do the thing and you will have the power." Sometimes it really is that simple. Just do the thing that you have been thinking about doing. Start the process of researching and testing right now. Do the thing you have been wanting to do forever and become the person you have been wanting to become.

The start is always the hardest. The first year, the first customers, the first website, the first million. The firsts are always the hardest, but starting and doing the thing now will give you the power later. More power to deal with more firsts. More knowledge and experience to use with the next first.

The night that the idea of my largest venture to date came about, I went and started working on it right away. I didn't wait for someone else to help me, I didn't wait for anyone else to invest in it to be able to get the first one done.  I just did it.  To this day, I still give my brother a hard time for not investing in that first project.  Luckily, I didn't sit around waiting for him to do so.

# CHAPTER 22
# QUICK TIPS

- Do the Thing and you will have the power.

- Planning is good, but over planning and overthinking is the death of productivity.

- Stop planning and start doing. There is great power in action.

- Once you start working, what needs to be done will become more and more clear.

- The start is always the hardest. Get over that first hurdle and you will be empowered to do more.

# CHAPTER 23:
# SET GOALS

**M**y brother and I set goals for our business every year and write them down in detail, yet we still manage to veer away from them throughout the year. We literally just said this year that we need to come back to this document x amount of times this year to ensure that this does not happen again. Setting goals seems so easy, it's following up on those goals that is much harder.

It's true what they say, "you must set goals and put them out into the universe for them to come true." Some people just say them or think them but the best tactic for achieving those goals is to write them down and revisit them often. There is something about writing an idea down that makes it real.

Our first office (other than my bedroom) was in the basement of our grandparents' small tax office in Portland. That basement was filled with tons of old computers, CD duplication machines, magazines and CD covers. In 2010, we moved from that office in Portland to our new location in Miami which changed our lives forever.

Five years later we went back to that office in Portland and everything was exactly the way we had left it, nothing had been touched. There was a white-board on the wall where we wrote all our goals and to-do lists. That whiteboard had one word written on it in big writing, "MIAMI". We wrote that right when we got back from visiting Miami the first time for a conference. We knew when we returned that "MIAMI" was our goal. That one word on the whiteboard...that one goal...it changed our lives.

# CHAPTER 23
# QUICK TIPS

## Simple Goal Sheet Example:

Long Term Goals
1.
2.
3.

Actions Needed to Get There:
1.
2.
3.

Short Term Goals
1.
2.
3.

This Month's Actions:
1.

2.

3.

## This Week's Actions:

1.

2.

3.

## Other Goals:

1.

2.

3.

# CHAPTER 24: FIND
# A REASON

easons, or what some people call "the why" are just as important as goals. They are often written down with the goals to keep them aligned. These are the reasons why you need to hit your goals. Why are those goals that you wrote down so important to you? Your reasons are going to keep the fire burning inside of you to attain those goals every time you look at them again.

Your reasons can also change over time and that is perfectly fine. The reason at the top of my list today did not even exist 4 years ago; my sons. Reasons can constantly change as can your goals and they should be revisited and updated. Long-term goals (dreams) and yearly goals are a bare minimum to keep up with, while also updating your current "reasons why" when you revisit them.

Your reasons why should be more than just monetary success, because it's going to take more than that to keep pushing you through the rainy days. Even if it means having financial freedom for a specific reason, to help a certain person or cause, then write that down. Really get down to the root of why you want to be a successful entrepreneur.

By the time I was a teenager, I was so fascinated by business that being a successful entrepreneur was my reason. The act of being "successful" itself is what fueled me to chase after the life of an entrepreneur, knowing that if just one idea worked then that would be a success to me. That was my reason why.

These days, my "why" is still the same for the most part. The spirit of entrepreneurship is more ingrained in my blood than ever and that gives me joy every day. However, my two children have become the reasons behind accomplishing those goals that are written on my goal sheet. To provide for them and give them the best life possible. Reasons for motivation can change. When they do, you should update your goal list, so you have something powerful pulling you towards those goals.

# CHAPTER 24
# QUICK TIPS

- Find the reasons why you want to achieve your goals and write them down with your goals.

- Your reasons why will keep you moving towards your goals in the hard times.

- Find reasons beyond money such as family, friends, charitable causes, proving people wrong, living your dream, etc.

- What will it feel like to achieve your goals? Picture it in your head and bring it to reality.

# CHAPTER 25:
# CREATE VALUE

As an entrepreneur, our income and success is tied directly to the businesses that we create and operate. A business only generates income and profits by bringing value to the marketplace, so as entrepreneurs our only way to make income is to create value out of nothing. This is important to keep in mind as you ride down the road of entrepreneurship.

When you are not making the income needed, it is time to look in the mirror and be honest with yourself about the value that you are bringing to the marketplace. The market is an amazing place that is brutally honest and will hit you square in the face with the truth of the value that you and your business are creating. The good news is, when you are bringing needed value to the marketplace it rewards you with the same tenacity that it was hitting you with when you were down.

It's an amazing feeling...to create money out of thin air with an idea. An idea that you and your team work hard to bring to life. An idea that is awarded value in the marketplace. That is what makes all the hard times worth it for an entrepreneur.

In my years of developing as an entrepreneur, I have begun to look at creating value differently. I understand now that value being created in the marketplace is great and will reward your company with gross income. I also understand, however, that gross income does not necessarily create value for your business.

Once value is brought to the marketplace and gross revenues are generated, the value of your company comes when you can systemize your processes and cut as many expenses as possible. Net Profit is most often and easily generated by cutting expenses of already systematized revenues of gross income.

To expand on the specifics of creating value in the marketplace, I would refer you to listen to some of the late Jim Rohn's speeches. He has some great motivational speeches that will get your mind racing about bringing value to the marketplace and becoming more valuable as a person. The book that I had mentioned earlier *Blue Ocean Strategy* is also a great place to learn more about the concepts of creating value in the marketplace and optimizing for profits.

# CHAPTER 25 QUICK TIPS

- Bring value to the marketplace and the marketplace will reward you.

- Listen to speeches from the late great Jim Rohn on creating value

- Once value is created, replicate that value to create as much gross income as possible

- Once gross income increases and plateaus, systemize and cut expenses to create profits.

# CHAPTER 26: FIND A MENTOR

Almost every business book I've read has touched on having a mentor and I'll tell you what...I completely agree. My mentors have been vital to my success. I have had a few throughout my career starting with Jason Hadshian, author of *How I Left My Job and Made It in the Music Industry.*

From the moment I met Jason at an event, he literally grabbed me by the shoulder and turned me around to introduce me to someone he thought I needed to know in the industry. By the time the event was over, he had introduced me to every person at that event and increased my network by tenfold. I didn't understand at the time what he was doing or why he did it, but he had become my mentor and that relationship has lasted 12 years.

That relationship with just one of my mentors has led to the ability to manifest multiple ventures into reality. That one person I met at one event in New York changed everything. He has since been a big brother type to look up to and ask for advice.

I had other mentors throughout my years in the music business, one of which is a world-famous DJ named Bigga Rankin. He has also been a "big brother" to me since we met at a conference in Miami in 2011. He is another mentor that I met at a networking event which shows the importance of networking and going to conferences and trade shows.

Bigga really embodies the philosophy that if you help enough other people get what they want, you can have everything that you want. He has helped so many people in the industry, that he will always be taken care of. When you give selflessly, you receive blessings back in droves. I am lucky enough to have some amazing mentors and for that I am grateful.

When it comes to the corporate and technology world, my actual biological brother Nick has been my mentor and business partner at the same time. Much of the knowledge and processes that I practice daily come from him. He is extremely bright and has been a blessing and mentor to me in many ways.

Each of my mentors have played a unique role in the development of my businesses and me as an entrepreneur. Finding a mentor is key...but you must create action until a mentor finds you. I got out there and put in the work myself. Which eventually led me to connect with people that were kind enough to take me on as a disciple. When the student is ready, the teacher will appear.

# CHAPTER 26 QUICK TIPS

- Mentors are key for advice and connections. You don't have the knowledge and connections that these experienced people do. Mentors are a shortcut to the learning curve.

- Immerse yourself in your industry at events and conferences, a mentor may be waiting for you at these events.

- You can have mentors that you don't know in person. Reading books and watching speeches can be a mentorship. Pick a mentor and learn from their advice and experience.

- If someone is kind enough to mentor you,

they believe in you. Never forget that or take it for granted.

# CHAPTER 27:
# CONQUER FEAR

I t seems crazy to me that people fear becoming an entrepreneur. They fear working for themselves and controlling their income, whether big or small. People actually fear this. I couldn't understand why people would be scared of something so amazing. I realize now it isn't being an entrepreneur that they fear, they fear themselves.

The fear of being an entrepreneur is being scared that you will not work as hard as you need to, to be successful. That is why most people work for someone else, for the safety of not having to face that fear. They don't want to take the leap of faith and rely on themselves to do the things it takes to get the power.

People want a nice warm job with a guaranteed paycheck. Some people have a family or obligations and do not want to risk being able to provide for them, so they have a guaranteed paycheck. That is great for people who want to succeed in that world, but that is not the world for an entrepreneur. That world is torture for a true entrepreneur to endure.

Don't get me wrong, there is nothing wrong with having a job. The world revolves around people having jobs. My own businesses revolve around our staff having jobs and I hope they enjoy their experiences with us. However, some people are just not made for that and if you are reading this book that probably includes you. Some of us are just entrepreneurs by design.

For those that want to reach for the stars to control their own destiny, they must conquer the fear. They must learn to harness the fear of failure and turn it into a fuel to shoot themselves to new heights of success. They must learn how to take risks.

# CHAPTER 27 QUICK TIPS

- Fear of being an entrepreneur is fear of not working hard enough. Overcome this fear with hard work.

- If being an entrepreneur is what you truly desire, don't be scared to take the leap of faith.

- Turn the fear of failure into the fuel that propels you to succeed.

# CHAPTER 28:
# TAKE RISKS

Having to take a risk is the gift and curse of being an entrepreneur. With every risk comes the chance of being knocked back down to where you started. You see, with entrepreneurs we are never really safe where we are. We are constantly taking risks and can lose everything in the blink of an eye.

There are countless stories of people who have had business empires and lost everything, sometimes even overnight. However, there are just as many stories about people who managed to get it back and then some, because they were never afraid to risk it all. This is a risky game, and you have to put up your bet to roll the dice.

Keep in mind that money itself is not real, it is just a value that we give to a piece of paper. The only value in money is the value that we see in it, the value that we assign to it. Money comes and goes but your knowledge, experience, network, and tools as an entrepreneur will remain with you. You are your most valuable asset as an entrepreneur, no matter how financially successful you become.

When you must take a big risk, just remember this; money is not real and is simply a tool to get what you want. Take calculated risks and do your research, but when the time comes, be ready to pull the trigger. Risk it if you need to, it won't kill you. You are going to have to sacrifice in this life of being an entrepreneur.

# CHAPTER 28 QUICK TIPS

- Don't be afraid to risk your money for what you believe in, you can always make it back.

- Your biggest asset as an entrepreneur is not the money you have to risk; it is the value within you.

- Take calculated risks and do your research, but when the time comes, pull the trigger.

# CHAPTER 29:
# SACRIFICE

How can you get something new in life if you are not willing to sacrifice something else? How can you get the time to spend on your business ventures if that time isn't being sacrificed from somewhere or someone else? The answers are simple, it's just not possible. You will have to sacrifice to turn your dreams into realities.

Your friends, family, and your romantic relationships will be sacrificed to some extent through the entrepreneurial process. If sacrifices did not have to be made, then wouldn't everyone be an entrepreneur? In his famous "Prime The Pump" speech, the late Zig Ziglar explains the concept of sacrifice so simply and brilliantly. He says "Isn't it true that if you could become a Medical Doctor by six weeks of summer school that the rewards would be almost minimal or nothing, and how many patients would you have?"

Sacrifice is what creates the value and separates us

from the rest of the world. Being afraid to take risks and make sacrifices is exactly what keeps people working jobs that they don't like their entire life. Sacrifice is the grit of the entrepreneurship hustle, it is something we all know too well and have to accept as the price we pay to live our dreams.

Are you ready to sacrifice your free time? Your downtime? Your time with your spouse or children? As a young person in the prime of your life, are you ready to sacrifice the parties and gatherings with your friends? Are you ready to sacrifice money you might normally spend on dinner or a movie and use it to invest in a new idea? Are you ready to eat ramen noodles for years before your business pays you enough for a decent meal?

These are the sacrifices that entrepreneurs make on a daily basis around the world. These are sacrifices that the non-entrepreneurs are not willing to make. "Successful people do what unsuccessful people are not willing to do." - Jim Rohn

# CHAPTER 29
# QUICK TIPS

- In order to get something new, you must sacrifice something old.

- You will sacrifice time from other people and activities. This is a fact of entrepreneurship that should be understood going into it.

- If being an entrepreneur did not take sacrifice, then everyone would be one. The sacrifice is what creates the rewards.

- Remember that successful people do what unsuccessful people are not willing to do.

# CHAPTER 30: ENDURE

Enduring entrepreneurship over a long period of time is something I'm still learning how to do. You know what they say, "More money, more problems" and I have definitely found that quote to be true. The more you have to lose, the more complicated and trickier this whole entrepreneur deal becomes.

Are you hurting one business by starting another new one? Is one business at risk legally from something that could happen to another business? Do you have the staff to run a new business? Do you even have the staff to run your current businesses?

An even more important question is...are your businesses able to endure time and run without you present constantly? Some would say that you are not an actual entrepreneur if you cannot create businesses and get them to the point of running themselves without you so that you can move on to the next venture. This is one that my brother and I have been improving but still struggle with it to this day.

A great resource with tips on how to set up your

business to run in longevity without you is a book called *Build A Business, Not A Job!* by Dave Finkel and Stephanie Harkness. This book has really improved my understanding of the difference between owning a business and being self-employed by your business. Since reading the book, we have set up many systems and processes to get us closer to being the owner of the business, instead of self-employed servants to it.

Do we have what it takes to endure entrepreneurship in the long run and keep growing? Only time will tell for us, as it will for you. My suggestion is to start the clock ticking right now. Don't waste another second waiting to become what you have always wanted to be. If you truly want it, then make the choice to become everything that you have the power to be.

# CONCLUSION

Taking the 30 short chapters of this book and applying them to your life and business is up to you, I can only offer the advice within these pages. There are quick tip guides in this book to do everything from forming an LLC to setting goals, and they can all be used to get you to full-time entrepreneurship. It starts with writing down your goals and listing your reasons to achieve those goals. Then by making a commitment and a playlist of motivational speaking to ensure you have a positive attitude to attain those goals. Those first steps set in motion will ultimately take you the rest of the way.

Once you set your goals in motion with a positive attitude you must sincerely work as hard as you can. Find a partner that can balance your strengths and weaknesses. Use the resources around you to build a team or a business. Are there people that you already know that specialize in areas that can help you? Is there something that you can sell before you even buy it? Something that you can launch with minimal investment?

Research your costs and the competition before getting too far into something. Start simple and be open to where the marketplace takes you. Follow your efforts and reinvest your profits back into advertising and testing new ideas. Don't be afraid to take risks and keep testing, but never forget to stay focused on the little things that got you there.

If you are out there working your business, networking, and pushing your dream then everything will align in due time. Your network will grow, your knowledge will improve, and you will attract what you need to win. A mentor will find you when you show that you are ready to receive mentorship. Everything tends to work out if you get out there and make it work.

There will be sacrifices made when working hard enough to make a change. Relationships and hobbies may have to be pushed into the shade in order to give your dream the light it needs to survive. The time and energy to nourish your dream has to come from somewhere in your life so something will be sacrificed. The question you have to ask yourself is..."is it worth the sacrifice?" My answer to that question has always been yes.

Being an entrepreneur isn't for everyone but for those of us lucky enough to be one, it's truly a beautiful feeling. Living the lifestyle of being my own boss and controlling my own income has been the ultimate dream. I mean, after all, I have *Never Had a Job* in my life. ~

# ABOUT THE AUTHOR

As the CEO of a multimillion-dollar company he founded at 15 years old, Kyle Hiersche had an early start as an entrepreneur. By age 27, he was investing in commercial and residential properties and owned a nightclub on Miami Beach. As the owner of six companies and counting, Kyle has a plethora of experience as an entrepreneur to share with the world.

Nick Hiersche, his brother and business partner, graduated from the University of Oregon College of Business. During his time at school, he helped Kyle build an idea into a successful company. Nick and Kyle were later asked to speak to the entrepreneurship class at the University of Oregon.

Today at the age of 31, Kyle remains an Entrepreneur as well as an author, licensed Realtor, and a real estate investor. For more books and info from Kyle Hiersche, visit https://linktr.ee/kylehiersche

# QUICK TIP GUIDES

## Starting A Corporation:

1. File an LLC with your state (One page form with a small fee that can be done online)

2. File LLC with Feds to get you EIN Number

3. Use you EIN number to get a bank account, checks, debit card, etc.

4. Set up a PayPal account with your bank account, order a PayPal debit card

5. Build your business!

## Creating A Brand:

1. Come up with your brand name

2. Create your logo using Canva or other easy design program

3. Purchase your website domain on GoDaddy.com

4. Create an email address at that domain
5. Use the logo and email to create profiles on Facebook, Instagram, Twitter, TikTok, etc.

6. Link to your website on all social media profiles

7. Start promoting your brand!

## Creating A Website:

1. Purchase Website Domain on GoDaddy.com

2. Use a simple service such as SquareSpace, Wix or Wordpress

3. Promote, test, analyze, update and repeat!

## Recommended Reading:

- *The Richest Man in Babylon* by George Samuel Clason

- *Think and Grow Rich* by Napoleon Hill

- *The Slight Edge* by Jeff Olson

- *Build A Business, Not A Job!* by Dave Finkel and Stephanie Harkness

- *Blue Ocean Strategy* by W. Chan Kim and Renée Mauborgne

- *Rich Dad Poor Dad* by Robert Kiyosaki and Sharon Lechter

- *As a Man Thinketh* by James Allen

## Recommended Motivational Speakers:

- Jim Rohn

- Zig Ziglar

- Tony Robbins

- Gary V.

- Les Brown

- Brian Tracy

- John Earl Shoaff

# Recommended Viewing:

- *CNBC Titans* (CNBC)

- *The Profit* (CNBC)

- *Shark Tank* (ABC)

- *Billion Dollar Buyer* (CNBC)

- *The Men Who Built America* (History)

- *Bar Rescue* (Spike)

- *The Pitch* (AMC)

- *Bloomberg Risk Takers* (Bloomberg)

KYLE N HIERSCHE

[1] United States Small Business Administration Office of Advocacy Frequently Asked Questions 2019